P9-BZZ-361

Alice in Wonderland

GALLERY BOOKS
An imprint of W.H. Smith Publishers Inc.
112 Madison Avenue
New York, New York 10016

TWIN
BOOKS

It was a very hot summer day: not a cloud was to be seen up in the sky and bees were buzzing everywhere.

"I'm so hot!" Alice said, lifting up her long hair.

"We can rest for a while, if you want," her sister offered and they sheltered from the sun under the shade of a big tree. Alice climbed up to the biggest branch and comfortably sat there while her sister reclined against the trunk. She took a book out and Alice wondered what to do while her sister was reading. Would the pleasure of making a daisy-chain be worth the trouble of getting up and picking the daisies?

Suddenly a white rabbit with pink eyes ran by quite close to her. She'd never seen anything quite like it. The Rabbit actually wore a waistcoat and a red jacket!

"Oh dear! Oh dear! I shall be too late!" the Rabbit said to himself.

"Wait for me," Alice called as she jumped down from the branch.

"I'm terribly late!" the Rabbit said and he didn't even stop to look at Alice. He carried a very big watch that he took out of his waistcoat pocket. Alice ran across the field after the Rabbit.

"Where are we going?" she shouted, but the Rabbit didn't answer.

Alice followed him anyway, but suddenly the Rabbit vanished. Fortunately Alice was just in time to see him pop down a large rabbit-hole under the hedge.

A moment later Alice had
jumped down into the hole.
She never thought about
how she would get out again.
Her dress puffed up like a
balloon and she fell and fell.
Either the well was very deep
or she was falling very
slowly. She had lots of time
to see what was around her
and to wonder what was
going to happen next. After
a long time, she finally
reached the bottom.

Alice looked up overhead but everything was very dark. In front of her was a long tunnel. The White Rabbit was still in sight, hurrying along. Alice started running at once to catch the Rabbit. She wanted to ask him so many questions. Before turning the corner, the Rabbit looked back to check if she was still following. Then Alice turned the corner and found herself in a big hall lit by lamps, but with no windows and no sign of the White Rabbit.

Alice examined the hall carefully and during her investigation she came upon a low curtain. Behind it was a little wooden door painted blue. She knocked, but no one opened it. "Little Rabbit, will you open the door?" she pleaded.

She heard the Rabbit mutter "I don't have time, I'm late!" Then she noticed that there was a tiny lock to the door.

She tried looking through the lock and she saw the loveliest garden you could ever dream about!

13

The lock guessed what Alice was thinking and said "You're much too big, my dear, you'll never be able to go through!" and then it began to laugh. But Alice didn't give up so easily. She looked around again and then she noticed that there was a table in the middle of the hall. She moved closer and saw a little bottle on it. Round the neck of the bottle, there was a label with the words "Drink me." Alice began to taste it and, as she liked it, she drank the whole bottle.

"What a strange feeling!" Alice said and she noticed that she had become so tiny that she was now smaller than the bottle. The table looked gigantic. How would she manage to get down? Then she realized that now she would be able to get through the little door.

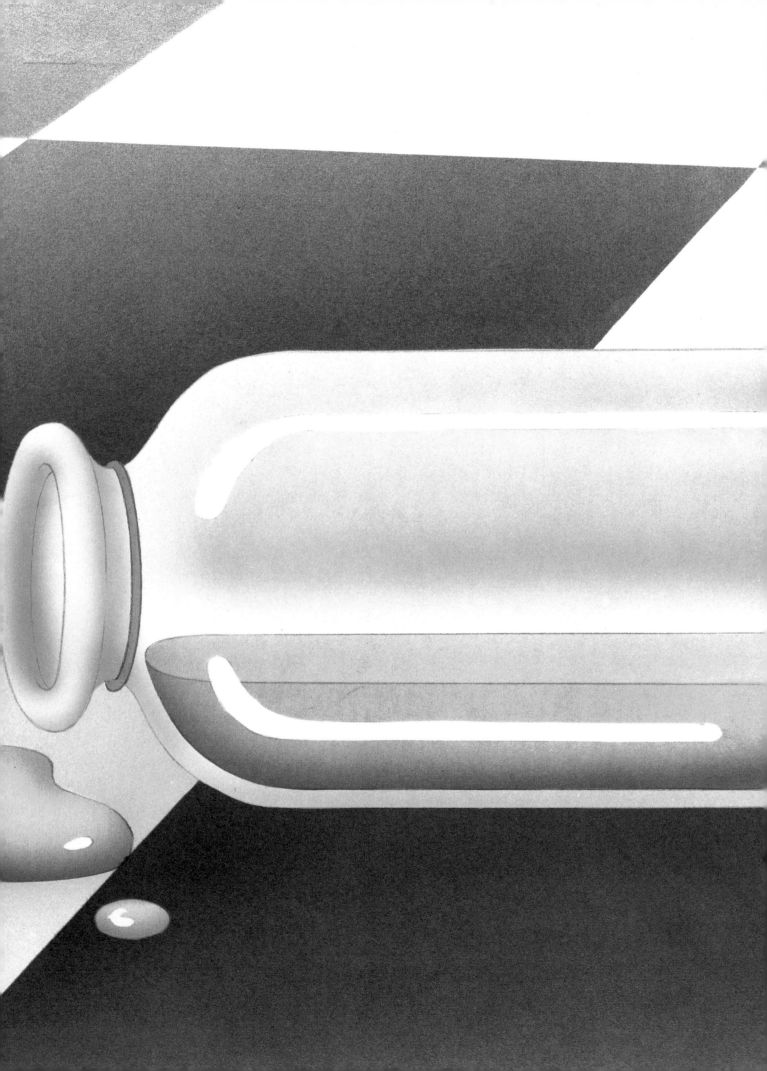

Alice got down off the table, which took a long time because she was so small, but when she got to the door, she discovered she had forgotten to take the key to the lock. It was still on the table, way out of reach. Alice tried her best to climb up one of the legs of the table, but it was too slippery. She was beginning to despair of ever succeeding when she noticed a box under the table. She found a small cake inside bearing the words "Eat me."

The cake tasted rather good, but when Alice looked at her hands, she saw them getting bigger and bigger.

"Good-bye feet!" she said as her feet seemed to move farther and farther away from her. The hall looked small and the ceiling very close. "Oh dear! I'm so big now that I'll never be able to go into the garden!" she said. Alice had turned into a giant!

When she realized that she was trapped in the room and would probably never be able to get out again, Alice burst into tears. She cried and cried and, since she was now a giant, she cried giant tears.

"If you keep crying, we'll all drown!" the lock said. "You would be better off thinking a little," it added.

Alice listened to this good advice and, looking around, she found that there were a few drops left in the bottle. She drank them, hoping that she would return to her natural size. Very soon she had not only begun to shrink, but she was so small that the tears she had shed appeared like a salt-water ocean.

"I wish I hadn't cried so much!" said Alice as she began swimming towards the little door. She was so small now that she was like a tiny insect on the surface of the water. Fortunately she had learnt to swim and she managed to reach the door.

When Alice got to the other side of the door, she could see land. A big party of animals was standing there. She swam over to the bank and asked them if they had seen a white rabbit go by.

Two fat little men came forward, saying "There isn't any White Rabbit here, but we are Tweedledee and Tweedledum, at your service!"

"Who are these two?" wondered Alice. "Probably twins. They look cheerful enough, but don't seem to want to listen to what I have to say."

All they cared about was talking and bragging. "Shall we tell her a story or a poem?" Tweedledee asked. "Let's have a poem. I'm sure she'll be delighted to hear our poem!" Tweedledum decided. Alice was rather bored but she didn't know how to get away from them.

"The Walrus and the carpenter, a poem written by Tweedledee and Tweedledum and by Tweedledum and Tweedledee" announced the twins speaking together.

"I don't think I'll understand much if you talk at the same time," Alice said.

"How do you expect us to tell a story if you interrupt all the time," Tweedledee and Tweedledum answered. "Besides we both made it up, so we absolutely must say it together." One had a low voice while the other one had a very shrill voice, so there was soon a horrible noise.

Alice waited until the twins started fighting and were so absorbed that they didn't even notice that she was leaving. She walked a while and then she saw a magnificent garden with pretty flowers and fountains. She felt happy and almost carefree. There was a house, the most charming house she had ever seen, just in front of her. Then the shutters were opened and who was there? No-one but White Rabbit!

"Wait for me," Alice shouted. "Am I on time for the appointment?" she asked.

The Rabbit came down to open the door, but he
didn't seem in the least surprised to see Alice. He was as
elegant and agitated as ever and instead of saying 'hello,'
he began scolding her: "Why Mary Ann, what are you
doing out there? Run home this moment and fetch me
a pair of gloves and a fan! Quick, now!" Alice was
too frightened to argue. She ran off in the direction the
rabbit had pointed.

"He mistook me for his housemaid," she said to
herself as she was running.

She found the Rabbit's bedroom. It was a neat little room with pictures of flowers and animals. She didn't have time to day-dream very long because she heard the Rabbit's voice calling to her from downstairs. "My gloves, my gloves, Mary Ann! I'll be late for my appointment!"

"Oh that Rabbit isn't any fun! He keeps repeating the same things over and over again. Where did he put his gloves?" Alice said to herself, but searching on the chest of drawers, instead of gloves she found a box full of cookies. They looked very appetizing, so Alice took one and another one...

She had hardly finished
eating the second cookie
when she felt her head
pressing against the ceiling.
She had grown so big that
she couldn't fit in the house
anymore. She had to put one
arm out of the window and
her feet out of the doors.

The Rabbit started yelling
"A monster! There is a
monster in my house! Help!"

He was right to be scared by Alice, she was as big as a giant now and couldn't move at all because the walls were beginning to shake and soon the house would collapse. "Good gracious! One can't eat anything here without changing size like a telescope!" Alice thought.

A funny bird joined White Rabbit and began discussing what had happened. "Interesting! Very interesting! How did this giant get into your house?" he asked.

"I don't know, but that's not the problem. How shall we get him out?" the Rabbit replied.

"Well, we could try to make a fire and the monster will have to come out so he won't choke," the bird suggested.

The Rabbit couldn't make up his mind. Perhaps the monster would indeed come out, but how about the house? Would it survive? Meanwhile Alice had managed to put her hand out and with her fingers she felt some leaves. She pulled and there was a carrot. She hardly hesitated at all before eating it. It was only a matter of habit, growing and shrinking and she was getting used to it.

As soon as she had nibbled the carrot, she once more began shrinking.

As soon as she was small enough to get through the door, she ran out of the house. She saw the strange bird whose name was Dodo, he was very pleased with his plan and said "You see, wasn't I right? All you had to do to get rid of that monster was to ask my advice. Don't hesitate next time you run into a problem, I'll be glad to help you."

The Rabbit being relieved of his worry about the house remembered his appointment, saying "I'm positive I'll be late!" and there he was running again!

Alice started doing the same, it felt so good to be free again! Then an idea crossed her mind. "The Rabbit left without taking his gloves, and when he notices, he'll probably be mad at Mary Ann. Since he thinks I am Mary Ann, he'll be mad at me!" Alice decided that perhaps she should look for him and try to explain that she wasn't able to find the gloves and that she wasn't a monster. She was so tiny now that the grass seemed like a gigantic forest. She headed in the direction where the rabbit had disappeared.

Alice looked all around, at the flowers and at the blades of grass. Everything looked enormous.

The air was full of strange insects, when she looked closer, she could see that they were flying cookies or toast dripping with honey. "If only I could catch them!" she thought, but they flew away. Alice also saw toys flying; small transparent horses who looked like dragon-flies. Everything was so different that Alice had stopped being puzzled. It was like dreaming!

As she walked along, she bumped into a big mushroom. She stood on tiptoe and peeped over the edge of the mushroom. Her eyes immediately met with those of a large Caterpillar, sitting on top of the mushroom with its arms folded, quietly smoking a long hookah.

The Caterpillar looked at Alice for a while, then it took the hookah out of its mouth and addressed her in a slow and sleepy voice. "What are you doing here?"

Alice shyly replied "I'm looking for a White Rabbit with pink eyes."

The Caterpillar began to laugh. "You're not going to catch him with your short legs!" he said. "Rabbits run very fast."

"I know." Alice said. "I don't run very fast because I am so tiny now. But I used to be a lot taller."

"Perhaps we could make you grow again. One side of this mushroom will make you grow taller and the other side will make you grow shorter." Saying this, the Caterpillar disappeared.

Alice looked thoughtfully at the mushroom for quite a while, trying to decide which side was which. It was a very difficult question.

However, at last she made up her mind and bit off a piece of the mushroom.

"And now what will happen?" she thought. She had an answer to her question very soon: she grew so quickly that her head pushed through the top of the trees and she was looking out over the top of the forest, frightening the birds.

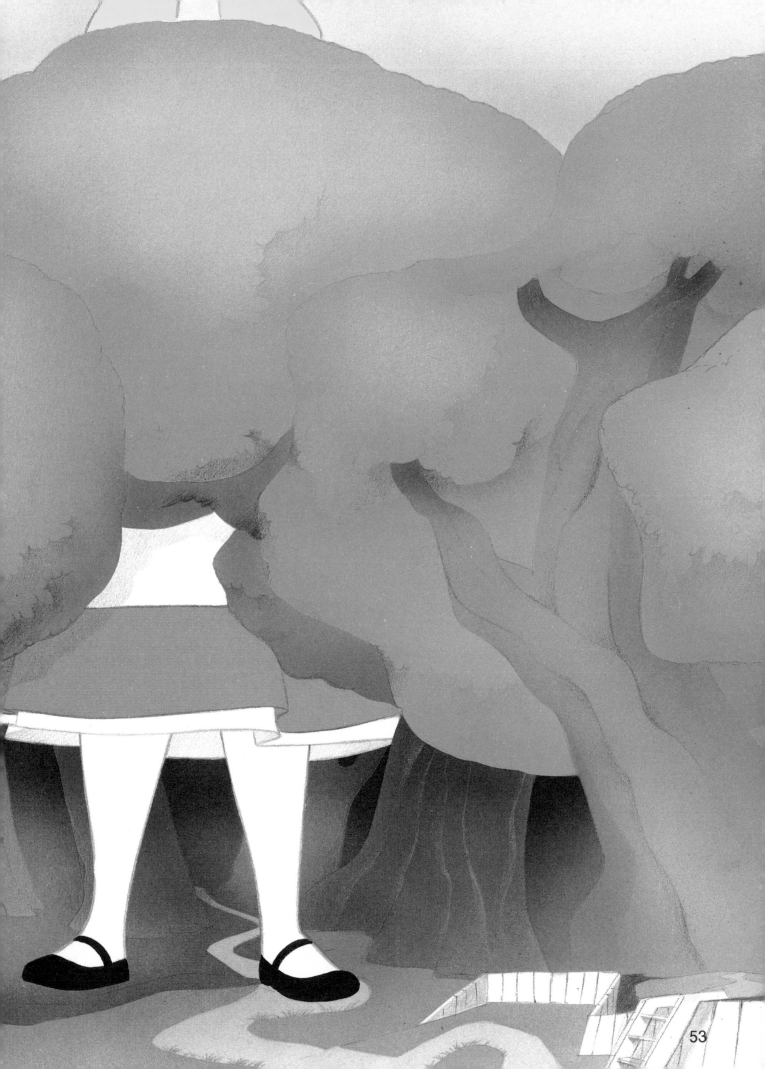

She had become a giant again! She could hardly see her feet. "Where have my shoulders disappeared to? And my hands, I can't even see them!" Alice said.

She was moving them about as she spoke, but nothing seemed to happen, except a little shaking among the leaves. "Even if I do find White Rabbit, he won't recognize me now!" she realized. A bird had confused her head with the top of a tree and he came to lay his eggs there. "Be off, this isn't a place for your nest." Alice told him. The bird was rather puzzled by this talking tree.

Alice was beginning to find it exhausting to change size all the time. She had had enough of being either a giant or the size of an ant. "How puzzling all these changes are! I wish I could go back to my real size!" she said. "But I can. All I've got to do is eat a very little more of the mushroom." So she nibbled at the bit of mushroom she had kept and brought herself down to nine inches high. She kept a piece, just in case she would need it later.

"Who knows, things are so very odd in this country!" she thought.

She was standing, noticing with pleasure that she was back to the size of an ordinary little girl, when she heard a voice behind her. She turned round in amazement and saw a big cat sitting on the bough of a tree just a few yards off. "Hello! Who are you?" she asked.

"I am the Cheshire Cat," he grinned. It looked like a good-natured cat but he had a lot of teeth, so Alice thought it was better to treat it with respect.

"Would you please tell me the way, which way I ought to go from here?" she asked again.

"That depends on where you want to get to," said the Cheshire Cat.

"I'm looking for a White Rabbit." she replied.

"What do you want to find that Rabbit for? I'll take you to my friend, the March Hare," said the Cheshire Cat. Alice followed him because she thought that a hare and a rabbit are almost cousins, so that perhaps she would find the Rabbit too.

"You'll also meet a Mad Hatter, he lives with the March Hare. We'll have tea together." the Cheshire Cat explained.

When they arrived, there was a big table set on the grass in front of the house. The March Hare and the Hatter were having tea at the table. There were several tea cups and a large teapot full of hot tea.

The March Hare was serving. The Hare and the Hatter greeted her, asking. "Is this your birthday?" Alice was forced to say it wasn't, although she thought that they would be greatly disappointed. "Never mind, we were just about to celebrate your non-birthday!"

"My what?" Alice asked.

"Your non-birthday. You only have one birthday. All the others are non-birthdays, so that gives us a lot more opportunities to have fun and celebrate," the Hatter explained.

Alice decided she might as well enjoy this unexpected party. The March Hare rushed to serve her some tea but he bumped into the Hatter who spilled his tea on his coat and on his bow-tie. "The tea is very strong, it will calm you down," he said. Alice was quite positive it was the opposite but she didn't even venture to try to convince him. "Let's have a song to celebrate this young lady's non-birthday!" announced the Hatter.

"Twinkle, twinkle, little bat!
How I wonder what you're at.
Up above the world you fly,
Like a tea-tray in the sky.
Twinkle, twinkle!"
When he had finished his song, he took his hat off and uncovered a big birthday cake with a candle.

Boom! Suddenly the cake exploded and Alice was covered with chocolate cream. The Hatter and the March Hare found this extremely amusing and burst into laughter.

Alice, who by that time had had enough of these two, left at once. Unfortunately, it was not easy to know where to go. There were signs everywhere saying: "THIS WAY," "NO, THAT WAY," "UP HERE," "OVER THERE." She was very confused.

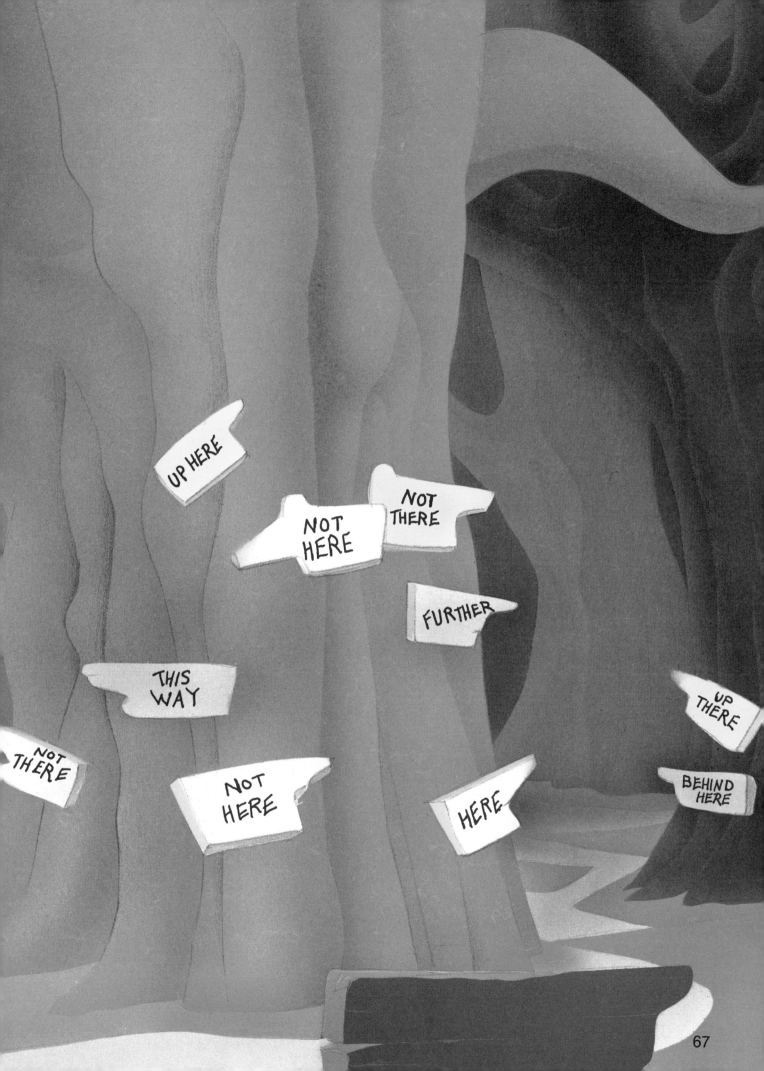

In fact, Alice was lost once more and could see no trace of the White Rabbit! She had seen so many strange things all day long that when a broom-dog got close to her, she was hardly surprised. The dog was sweeping everything in its way and after he had gone by, there was nothing left behind, not even a path. That's why Alice couldn't find her way.

She heard someone laugh right next to her and when she looked up she saw the Cheshire Cat, in a tree.

"Are you lost again?" he asked, "Is that your favorite occupation?"

"You're the one who got me lost," she protested. "You took me to a Mad Hatter, instead of showing me where the Rabbit had gone." Alice was very cross.

"You're not very pleasant, but I'm a good-natured cat and I'll help you anyway," the Cheshire Cat replied. "Follow me."

They walked down a little passage and then she found herself in the beautiful garden at last, among the bright flower-beds and the pretty fountains. A large rose tree stood near the entrance of the garden.

There were three gardeners busily painting the white roses red. As she went nearer, she saw the gardeners were shaped like playing cards. "Would you tell me," Alice asked timidly, "why you are painting these roses?"

"Well, miss, you see this tree ought to have been red. The Queen only likes red roses," they answered.

At that moment, one of the gardeners, who had been anxiously looking across the garden, called out "The Queen! The Queen!" The doors of the palace opened and a long line of soldiers came out. Like the gardeners they, too, were shaped like playing cards, in black and white or red and white.

Next came the courtiers, two-by-two. After these came the royal children, jumping and playing merrily hand-in-hand. The Knave of Hearts followed. He carried a cushion with the royal crown on it. Last of all came the Queen.

When the Queen of Hearts was level with Alice, she stopped and looked at her. "Who is this?" she demanded to know. The Knave of Hearts only bowed and smiled.

"My name is Alice, your Majesty," said Alice very politely, "I'm looking for a White Rabbit."

"A White Rabbit!" Nonsense! Do you know how to play croquet?"

"A little," Alice answered wondering what the game would be like. In fact she had never seen such a curious croquet ground before: the balls were live hedgehogs and the mallets live flamingos.

The courtiers started applauding. The Queen seemed to enjoy the game tremendously. "Very good!" she occasionally said. Alice tried her best to please the Queen, but it was rather difficult to play with live animals. Usually she managed to get the flamingo's body tucked away, but when she was about to hit the hedgehog with the flamingo's head, it twisted itself round and started to look up in her face. The Cheshire Cat, who hated the Queen, suddenly jumped on her back and tied the bottom of her dress to a flamingo's beak.

The Queen didn't notice this, but just as she was about to win, she lifted her arm up high and the flamingo held on so tight that she fell upside down. All that could be seen of the dignified Queen was two legs wiggling in the air. Everybody had a good laugh, even her husband the little King, who followed her around so devotedly.

When the Queen finally was able to get up, she was red as a lobster and she began to have a tantrum. "You're the one who is responsible. I shouldn't have trusted you, you're neither heart, nor club, nor spade, not to mention diamonds! You don't belong here!" she screamed at Alice.

"I didn't ask to be here and it isn't my fault!" Alice began, but she was immediately interrupted by the Queen.

"What's this? I'm the one who rules here. Take her away and off with her head!" the Queen shouted.

"She must be tried first,"
the King timidly said. The
Queen was astounded that
he had dared to speak.

"Let her be tried then!" she
said reluctantly.

They all immediately went to court. Alice was very impressed. The Queen got up on a high throne and began addressing the audience: "We are here to judge this girl who is guilty of the crime of treason. She will have her head cut off. That's my sentence!" When she finished, she sat down.

"But that's not a trial," the little King said. "There must be witnesses and the jurymen must decide what the sentence will be."

"Who is the Queen here?" demanded her Majesty. No one else dared to speak up for Alice.

Alice understood that if she wanted to get out of this unpleasant situation, she should act for herself, as the little King would not be able to do much for her. She started thinking very hard about what to do. Then, fortunately, an idea crossed her mind: "All I have to do," she exclaimed, but as quietly as she could, "is to eat some of the mushroom I kept in my pocket and then I'll be very big again and I will scare them off!" She immediately bit a piece of the mushroom and she began growing and growing.

The whole gathering was panic-stricken when they saw that Alice was so big. Everyone rushed to the exit and although the Queen shouted "Off with her head!" nobody listened to her anymore.

"Who cares for you?" Alice said. "You're nothing but a pack of cards!" And with these words, she saw the pack rise up into the air and then fall down again.

Alas! That wasn't the end of Alice's adventures. She was much too big to go through the door, so she had to eat a piece of the mushroom to get back to a small size. It was indeed perfect to go through the door, but her enemies, seeing her back to a miniature size, started running after her.

The Queen was screaming at the top of her voice: "Get hold of her! I want her head to be cut off!" Luckily, the little King managed to help Alice by showing her a back door and she finally escaped.

She thought she was safe at last, but in fact she was trapped in a maze. She could hear the pounding feet of the soldiers searching for her. "How will I find the exit?" she wondered. Alice felt like giving up everything and going to sleep. She closed her eyes.

She could still hear the Queen's harsh voice far in the distance, but faintly, as if it was in a dream. She found herself surrounded by a cloud and had the impression of seeing the Mad Hatter, the White Rabbit and the March Hare go by in the distance. She couldn't hear what they said anymore. She whispered in a sleepy voice, "White Rabbit. Wait for me! Off with her head!"

"Wake up, Alice dear! You've been sleeping a long time!" Alice's sister gently woke her up.

"I've had such a strange dream!" said Alice and she told her sister of her strange adventures as they walked back home. "You know in Wonderland white rabbits have watches in their waistcoat pockets and they run because they're late for their appointments."

Published by
Gallery Books
A Division of W H Smith Publisher Inc.
112 Madison Avenue
New York, New York 10016
USA

Produced by
Twin Books
15 Sherwood Place
Greenwich, CT. 06830,
USA

Copyright © 1986 The Walt Disney Company

All rights reserved. No part of this book may be reproduced or transmitted in any form or by any means without written permission from the Publisher.

ISBN 0-8317-0287-7

Printed in Spain

1 2 3 4 5 6 7 8 9 10